Indianapolis Motor Speedway

INDIANAPOLIS MOTOR SPEEDWAY

W9-CAZ-568

Hall of Fame Museum

The Hall of Fame Museum on the grounds of the famed Indianapolis Motor Speedway, a National Historic Landmark since 1987, appeals to more than just the racing enthusiast. Displayed are more than 75 vehicles, including a number of Indianapolis winners and other classics of the "500," a variety of classic European sports cars and early Grand Prix cars, plus several vintage and veteran early-day passenger vehicles and motorcycles.

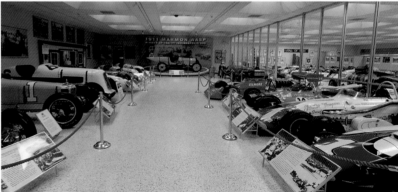

The city of Indianapolis was once one of the centers of the automobile industry, and at one time or another was home to such famous makes as Stutz, Duesenberg, Marmon, Cole and National, while from around the state one could add Studebaker, Auburn, Cord, Lexington, McFarlan, Overland, Haynes, Apperson and numerous others.

The winning cars of three of the first four Indianapolis 500-Mile Races are almost always on display, including the famed Marmon "Wasp" which won the very first "500" ever held, in 1911. This car, a single-seater, is believed to have been the first automobile ever to be equipped with a rearview mirror, this coming about when other participants during practice complained that without a riding mechanic, driver/engineer Ray Harroun represented a potential safety hazard.

In the Beginning

Although the collection and preservation of classic passenger cars had always been quite prevalent in this country, the same could hardly be said for racing cars. While retired competition cars tended to be cherished in the European countries from the very beginning, it was not really until the 1950s that racing cars in the United States began to receive the same kind of treatment, a notable exception being the Marmon "Wasp."

At a dinner in Indianapolis on the evening of May 27, 1947, just 18 months after he had purchased the Indianapolis Motor Speedway, Anton Hulman, Jr., expressed his dream for a museum and/or "hall of fame" to honor the accomplishments of outstanding individuals within motor sports.

Five years later, while Hulman was still concentrating his focus on the upkeep and improvement of the track, a Hall of Fame was created. It began as a joint project between the Contest Board of the American Automobile Association (AAA) in Washington, DC—then America's premier motor racing sanctioning body—and officials at the Edison Institute of the Ford Foundation in Detroit. The process of selecting names for induction began in 1952, but there was no "home," and attempts at obtaining classic racing cars for any kind of permanent display met with little or no success.

Karl Kizer, the museum's curator for over 25 years.

Perhaps surprisingly, it would not be until April of 1956 that the offices of the Indianapolis Motor Speedway would actually be located on the grounds themselves, all previous year-round business since 1909 having been conducted at a variety of addresses in the 400 block of North Capitol Avenue in downtown Indianapolis.

Tony Hulman, a man of vision.

The Indianapolis Motor Speedway Hall of Fame Museum in the late 50s.

In the fall of 1948, after 30 years of residence at 444 North Capitol, new owner Tony Hulman had decided to move the offices three blocks north to Karl Kizer's Century Tire building at 729. Kizer was a longtime enthusiast who had owned dirt-track cars in the 1920s and '30s and who had befriended many racers over the years by making the back part of his building available to them for storage and for working on cars. Three-time "500" winner Wilbur Shaw, who was now Hulman's track president and general manager, had been friends with Kizer for more than 20 years and the three of them would fantasize on hunting trips about the creation of a museum.

The new building was ready by early April, 1956.

On October 30, 1954, Wilbur Shaw died in a private plane crash near Decatur, Indiana, while returning from a business trip to Detroit. The following month, during a nostalgic conversation on another hunting trip, Tony told Kizer, "We'll do it." On July 25, 1955, ground was broken on the southwest corner of the Speedway property next to what, since 1909, had been the main entrance. Assisting in the first shovelful of earth was Tony's daughter, Miss Mari Hulman; Catherine "Boots" Shaw, Wilbur's widow; and Bob Sweikert, winner of the most recent "500." The plans for the single-story brick building called for offices in the west wing and the much anticipated museum to be located in the east wing. The offices were completed on April 7, 1956, and the museum portion, while never formally opened, began operating around the time of the first weekend of time trials in May, with Kizer the curator as "a dollar a year man."

Only six cars were on display at first, three lined up on each side of a long centrally located display of photographs and memorabilia. Karl Kizer was in possession of Fred Frame's 1932 winner and had it trucked over. The 1911-winning Marmon "Wasp" was another early acquisition as was Gordon Schroeder's Sampson "16," containing the very engine with which Frank Lockhart had tried, with tragic results, to capture the World Land Speed Record in 1928. Wilbur Shaw's 1939 and '40-winning Boyle Maserati, which had still been racing 10 years later, was ready for display after a painstaking restoration, as was the 1925 second-place-finishing front-drive Miller, once it had been considerably freshened up following years of lying in the back of a butcher's shop in South Bend, Indiana. The sixth car was Freddie Agabashian's 1952 pole-winning Cummins Diesel, temporarily on loan from the Cummins Engine Company.

The Museum Today

The current museum building was opened on April 5, 1976, coincidentally almost 20 years to the day after the opening of the original museum. The museum floor can comfortably exhibit 70 or 80 cars. Portraits of living members of the Hall of Fame adorn the west wall of the "500" Museum.

In 1955, a steeply banked 2.3-mile concrete oval was constructed at the Grand Prix track in Monza, Italy, which could either be linked in with the existing road course or used separately. The organizers soon created "The Race of Two Worlds" with the intention of having 10 leading Indianapolis cars and drivers take on 10 leading Grand Prix cars and drivers in a 500-mile race. Conducted, for safety reasons, in three 63-lap segments, the Monza 500 was held twice, the Grand Prix drivers shunning the event completely in 1957 but making a reasonable showing in 1958. The cars of Jimmy Bryan, overall winner in 1957, and Jim Rathmann, winner of all three segments in 1958, are normally on display with the event's trophy between them.

Indiana Built Cars

Before Detroit finally became established as the center of the American automobile, there were several extremely prolific cities, Indianapolis being among them.

In 1913, Indianapolis ranked second in terms of numbers of automobiles produced. Among the better known makes were Duesenberg (1920-37), Stutz (1911-35), Marmon (1902-33), Cole (1909-25), National (1900-24), American Underslung (1906-14), Premier (1903-26) and Marion (1904-15).

The state of Indiana was also home at various times to Studebaker (South Bend), Auburn and Cord (Auburn), McFarlan and Lexington (Connersville), Westcott (Richmond), Interstate (Muncie), Simplex (Mishawaka), Haynes and Apperson (Kokomo), Elcar (Elkhart), Great Western (Peru) and ReVere (Logansport). Much of the industry had either ceased or relocated by the mid-1930s, Studebaker surviving until 1963.

1917 Pathfinder

Indiana Built Cars

This particular 1927 Duesenberg Model "A" is quite unique because for many years it was Augie Duesenberg's personal transportation. It was still in his possession when he passed away in 1955.

**1927 Duesenberg
Model A**

1921/1922 Duesenberg

One of the greatest upsets ever in international motor racing took place on July 26th 1921, when four American Duesenberg racing cars were sent over for the French Grand Prix and one of them, driven by Jimmy Murphy, won the race. Held over the famed Le Mans course—two years before the first running of the 24-Hours endurance race—this marked the first occasion on which an international Grand Prix had been won by an American driver in an American car. In fact, it has only happened once since, when Dan Gurney won the 1967 Belgian Grand Prix in an Eagle. Shortly after returning home, Murphy purchased the car from the Duesenberg brothers and proceeded to remove the straight-eight Duesenberg engine and replace it with a straight-eight Miller. He won the 1922 Indianapolis 500, the first ever to do so from the "pole" position. The car was discovered 30 years later in very poor condition in Southern California by Murphy's old riding mechanic, Ernie Olsen, who arranged for it to be returned to Indianapolis where it was restored to the way it had appeared at the French Grand Prix.

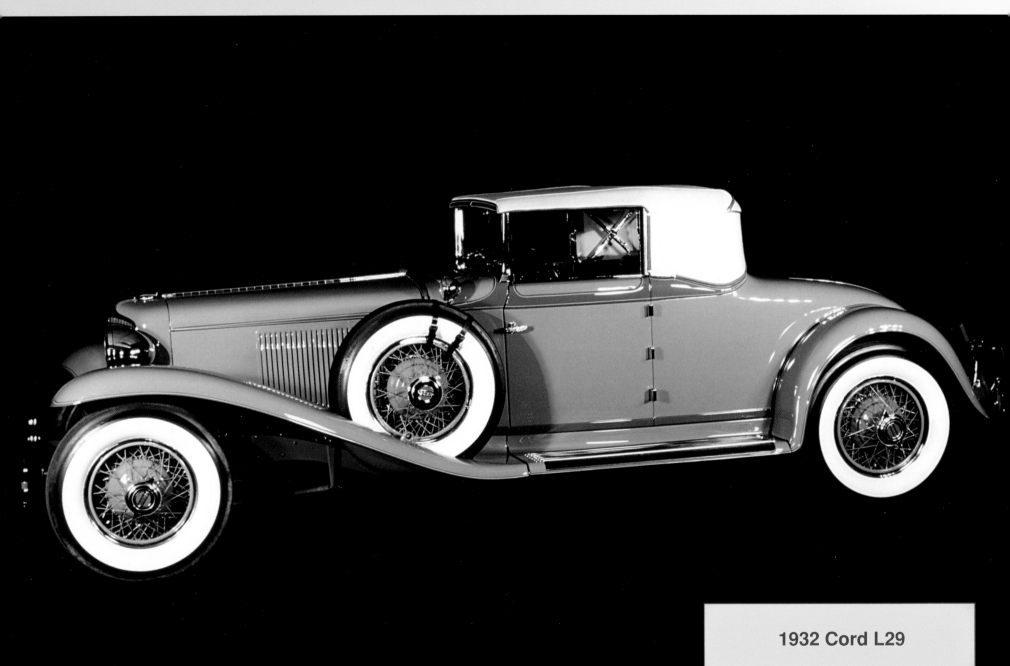

1932 Cord L29

was another fine Indiana-made car, its factory operating in Connersville in the
rt of the state between 1910 and 1925.

1925 McFarlan

1896 Reeves

1896 Benz

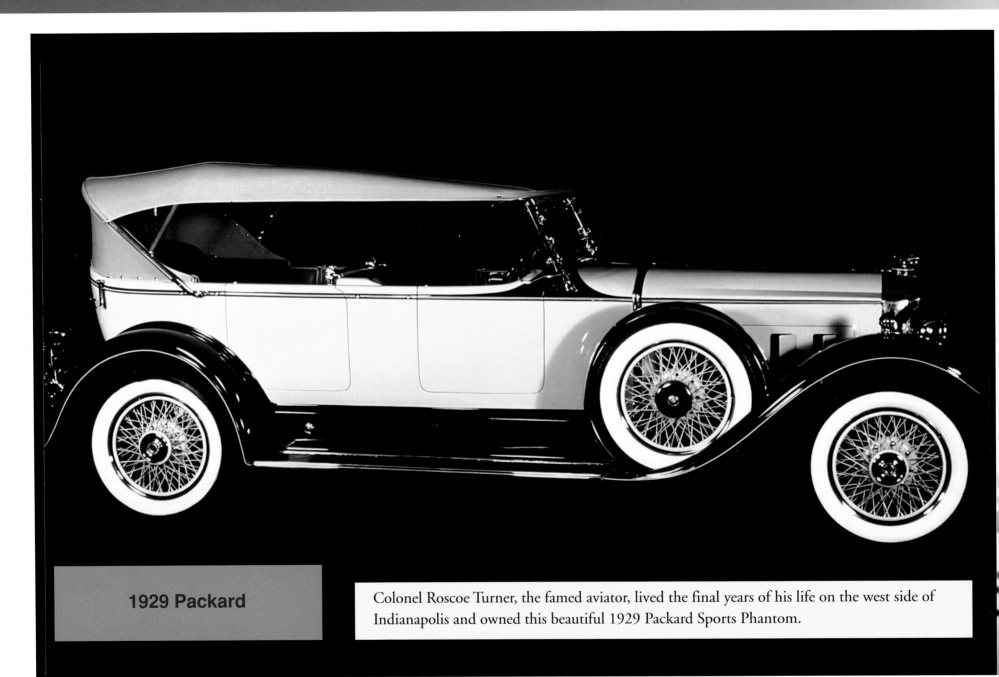

1929 Packard

Colonel Roscoe Turner, the famed aviator, lived the final years of his life on the west side of Indianapolis and owned this beautiful 1929 Packard Sports Phantom.

1932 Cadillac V-16

1927 Mercedes-Benz
Model S

1928 Mercedes-Benz
Cabriolet Limousine

1896 Leon Bollée

Sometime in the late summer of 1956, Chevrolet decided to go international sports-car racing with a team of special Corvettes. Encouraged by famed GM engineers Harley Earl, Ed Cole and Bill Mitchell, and with only a few months of lead time, project engineer Zora Arkus-Duntov set about trying to create a world beater. They planned to hire the two leading Grand Prix drivers of the day, Juan Manuel Fangio of Argentina and Stirling Moss of England, but Moss would not commit until he could be sure the cars would be ready in time and Fangio, who actually signed a contract, was released when time for testing ran out. A single car was taken to Sebring in March for American John Fitch and Italian Piero Taruffi, but a variety of minor problems forced it out after only a few laps. Even as this was taking place, the American Manufacturers Association was in the process of agreeing amongst itself to no longer support motorsports, thus ending the planned invasion of Le Mans and other European circuits before it even began.

1957 Chevrolet Corvette SS

19

Although this could easily be mistaken for being a sports car, it is actually a 1954 Mercedes-Benz W196 single-seat Grand Prix Formula One car, built at a time when rules did not yet preclude enclosing the wheels. Led by the great Juan Manuel Fangio to the World Championship in both 1954 and 1955, the Mercedes team would typically field its "streamliners" on fast circuits like Rheims (France) and Monza (Italy), but take more conventional open-wheel versions to the tighter road courses.

1954 Mercedes-Benz W196

1960 Maserati Type 61
"Birdcage"

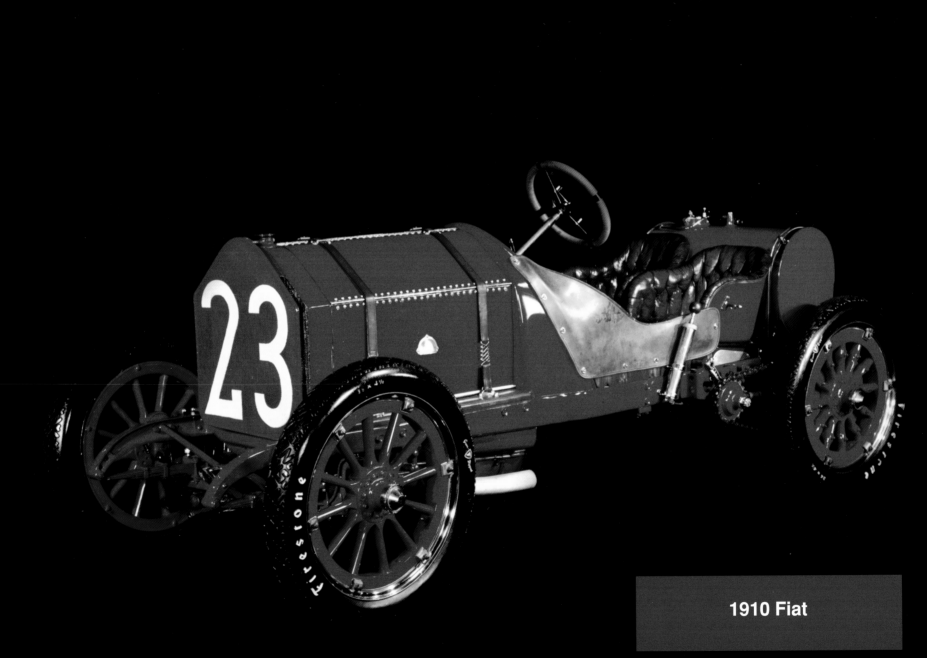

1910 Fiat

This Ferrari 250LM, privately entered by the North American Racing Team (N.A.R.T.), was driven to victory in the 1965 Le Mans 24-hours enduro by Masten Gregory of the United States and Jochen Rindt of Austria.

1965 Ferrari 250LM

1907 Itala

1906 Renault

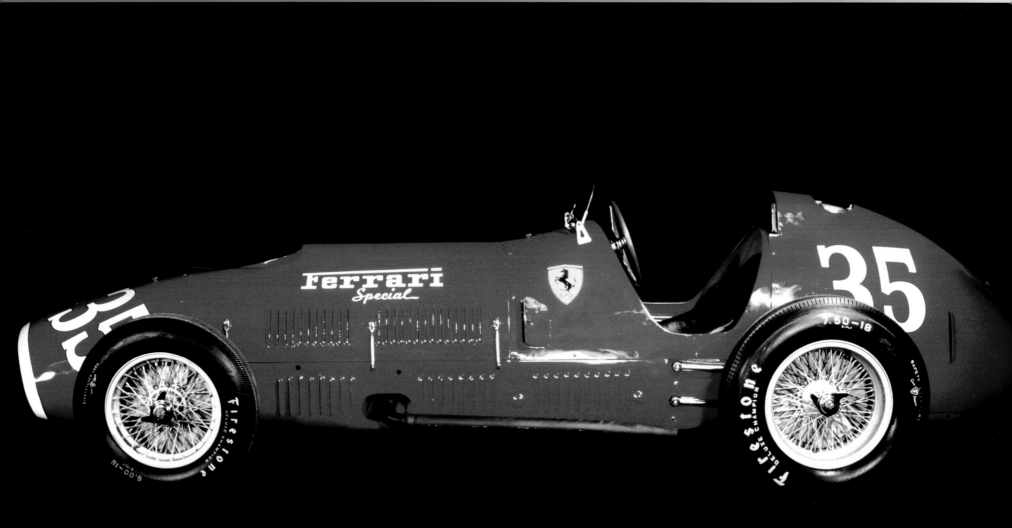

1952 Ferrari type-375

Long-time racing enthusiast Clark Gable attended the "500" as the guest of track owner Tony Hulman in 1947 and 1948. When the legendary actor returned for a longer stay in 1950 to shoot scenes for MGM's racing epic, "To Please A Lady," also starring Barbara Stanwyck, perfect host Hulman went out of his way to find a private car he knew Gable would thoroughly enjoy. Knowing Gable had recently taken delivery of a Jaguar XK-120 in Los Angeles—it appears briefly in a scene in the film—Hulman located and acquired the one seen here. In addition to being Gable's "drive-around" car for May, it was also featured in several parades, one taking place in Terre Haute with Hulman driving and Gable as his passenger.

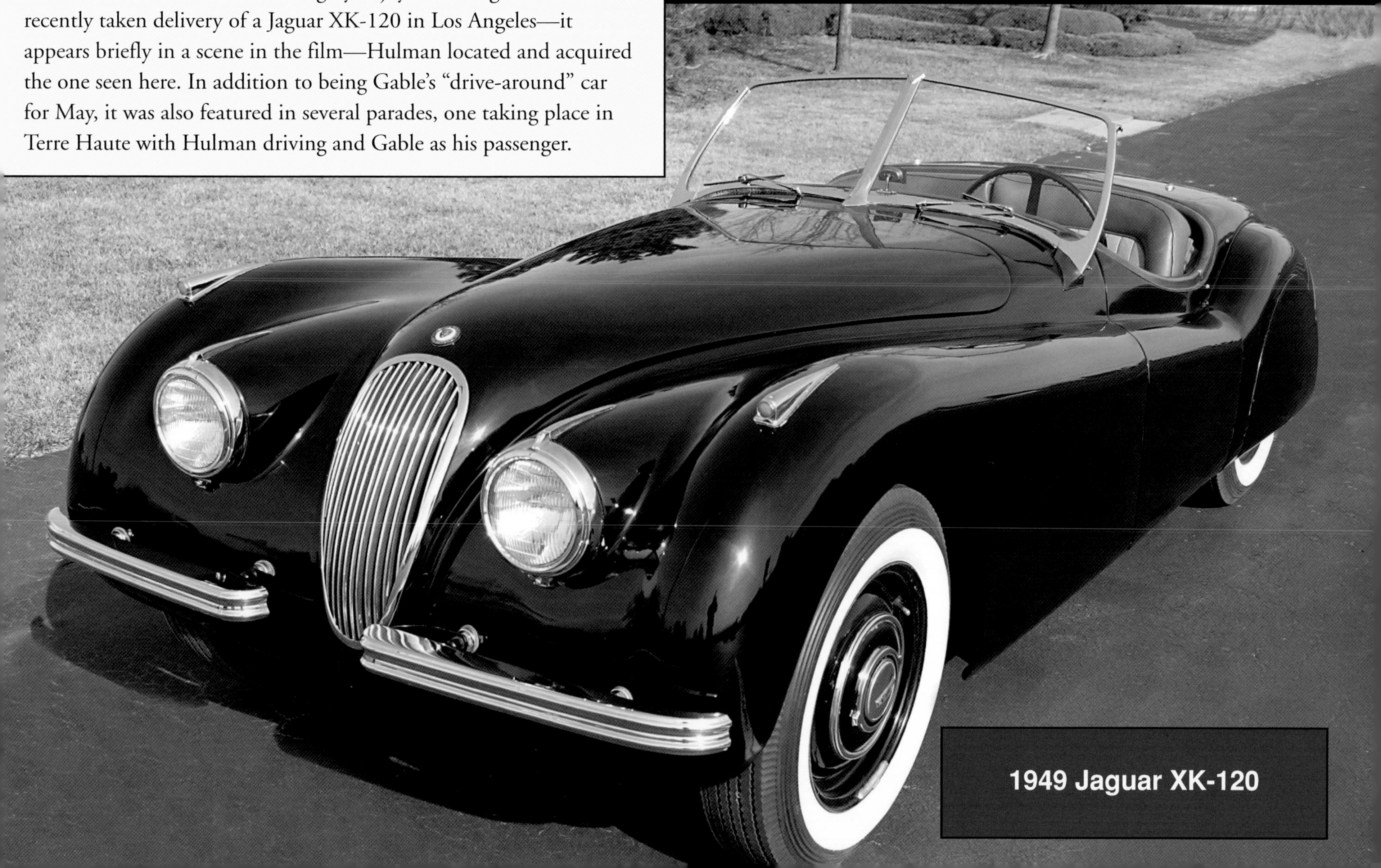

1949 Jaguar XK-120

**1938 Alfa Romeo
Type-308C**

1922 TT Bentley

The English Bentley company was barely three years old when founder W.O. Bentley decided to enter some sports-car races in 1922. After a team of four touring models had been entered for July's Tourist Trophy event on the Isle of Man, wealthy W. D. Hawkes decided to take one of them to Indianapolis. In spite of it being merely a stripped-down sports car, Hawkes completed the full 500 miles and finished 13th, rolling along at an average speed of 74.95 mph and making only one pit stop along the way.

First "500" Winner

The Inaugural Indianapolis 500 race was a huge success. The race was won in a time of 6 hours and 42 minutes (an average speed of 74.602 mph) by Ray Harroun, driving a racing version of the locally built Marmon passenger car. Because a number of the other participants had complained during practice that the car's streamlined single-seat design represented a safety hazard by having no provision for a riding mechanic, driver/engineer Harroun had been forced to come up with a solution. Remembering something he had seen on a horse-drawn taxi in Chicago seven years before, he rigged up four rods above the cowling to which he attached a three-by- eight-inch mirror, believed to have been the first ever used on an automobile.

Further history was made when Carl Fisher determined that forty cars were too many to dispatch from the traditional standing start. He decided it would be safer instead to have them follow his passenger car around for one unscored lap at about 50 mph and then release them to the flagman as he pulled into the pits. It is believed to have been the first mass rolling start for any automobile race anywhere in the world, and quite possibly the first use of a pace car.

1911
Marmon "Wasp"

Indianapolis "500" Winning Cars

A.J. Foyt was the first driver ever to win the Indianapolis "500" four times.

All four of his winning cars are part of the collection and are normally displayed next to each other.

**1961
Bowes Seal Fast
Trevis/Offenhauser**

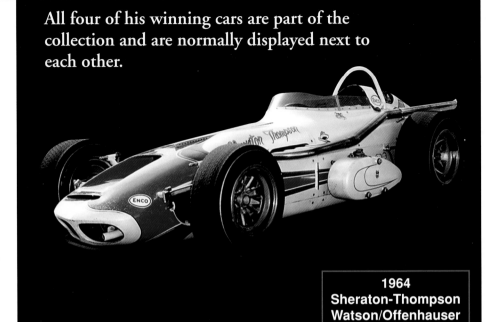

**1964
Sheraton-Thompson
Watson/Offenhauser**

**1967
Sheraton-Thompson
Coyote/Ford**

**1977
Gilmore Racing Team
Coyote/Foyt**

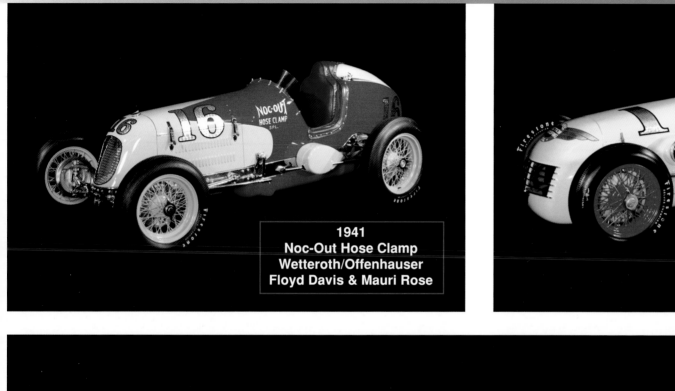

1941
Noc-Out Hose Clamp
Wetteroth/Offenhauser
Floyd Davis & Mauri Rose

1950
Wynn's Friction Proofing
Kurtis/Offenhauser
Johnnie Parsons

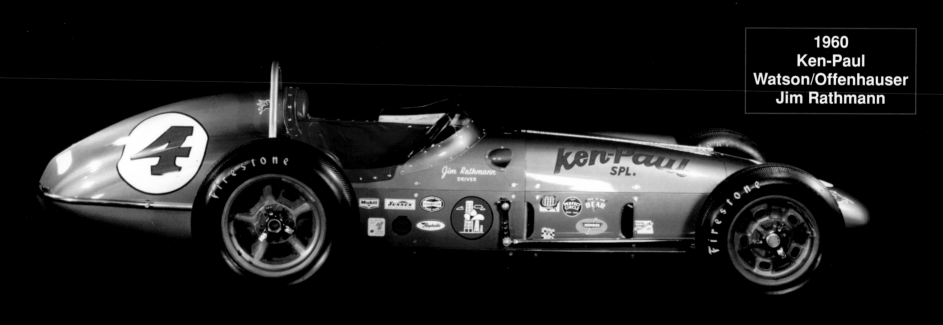

1960
Ken-Paul
Watson/Offenhauser
Jim Rathmann

Indianapolis "500" Winning Cars

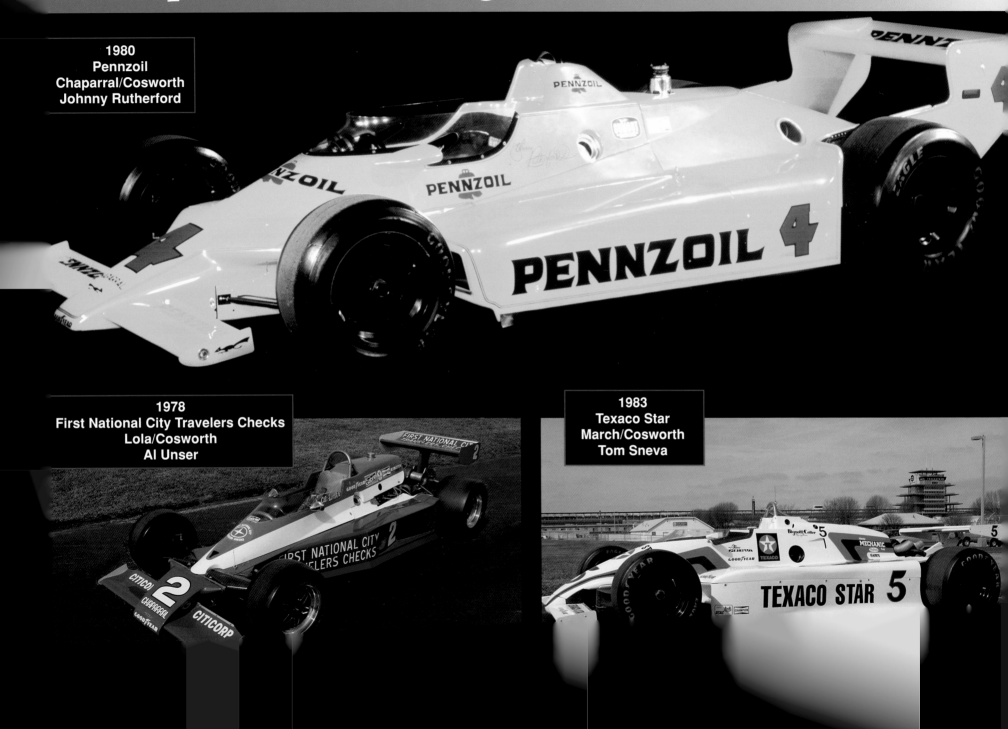

1980
Pennzoil
Chaparral/Cosworth
Johnny Rutherford

1978
First National City Travelers Checks
Lola/Cosworth
Al Unser

1983
Texaco Star
March/Cosworth
Tom Sneva

**1914
Delage
Rene Thomas**

**1912
National
Joe Dawson**

Indianapolis "500" Winning Cars

1962
Leader Card
Watson/Offenhauser
Rodger Ward

1968
Rislone
Eagle/Offenhauser
Bobby Unser

1947/1948
Blue Crown Spark Plug
Mauri Rose

1955
John Zink
Kurtis/Offenhauser
Bob Sweikert

1972
Sunoco
McLaren/Offenhauser
Mark Donohue

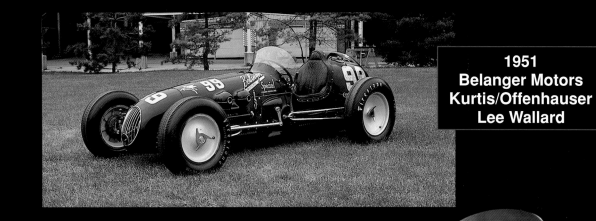

1951
Belanger Motors
Kurtis/Offenhauser
Lee Wallard

1928
Miller
Louis Meyer

1953/54
Fuel Injection
Kurtis/Offenhauser
Bill Vukovich

1957
Belond Exhaust
Salih/Offenhauser
Sam Hanks
(also won in 1958, Jimmy Bryan)

1982
STP Oil Treatment
Wildcat/Cosworth
Gordon Johncock

1963
Agajanian's Willard Battery
Watson/Offenhauser
Parnelli Jones

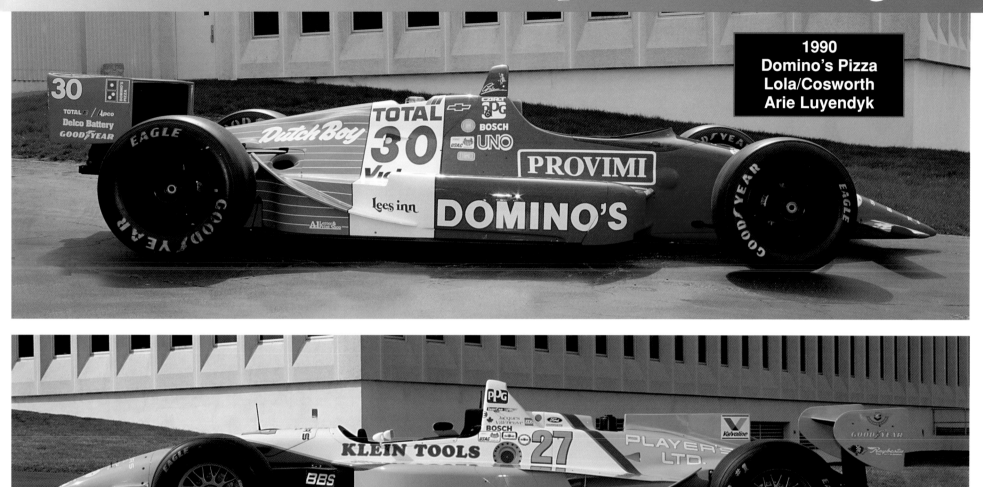

1990
Domino's Pizza
Lola/Cosworth
Arie Luyendyk

1995
Players, Ltd
Reynard/Ford Cosworth
Jacques Villeneuve

1938 Maserati 8CTF

Perhaps the most successful Indianapolis "500" car of all time, this 1938 eight-cylinder 3-liter (183-cubic-inch) supercharged Maserati won in 1939 and 1940 in the hands of Wilbur Shaw, the first occasion on which either a car or driver had won in consecutive years. Trying for three in a row, Shaw was leading at the three-quarter distance in 1941 when a wire wheel collapsed, causing the car to spin into the wall. Ted Horn drove it to third position in 1946 and 1947 and to fourth in 1948. It was 11 years old by the time Lee Wallard led several laps with it in 1949, and in 1950 it was used by eventual two-time winner Bill Vukovich for passing his "rookie" test.

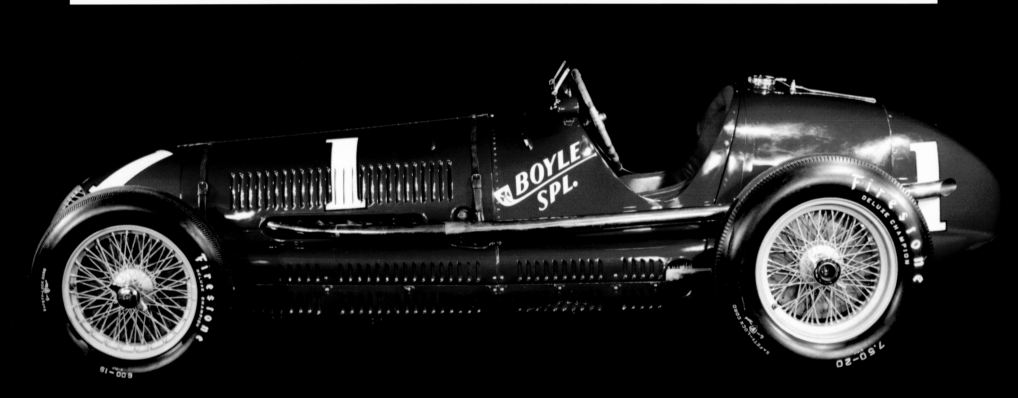

1939 & 1940
Wilbur Shaw

During the 1940s and 1950s, the extremely popular Novi racing cars had a following to rival that of just about any driver. Financed by industrialist Lew Welch of Novi, Michigan, and designed by Ed and Bud Winfield in collaboration with Leo Goosen, the Novi engine was an extremely loud and powerful supercharged V8. A Novi would invariably break track records and lead the race, but could never seem to win and more often than not would fail to finish. The highest placing ever was third in 1948 by the car seen here, driven by Duke Nalon, who also won the pole position with it in 1949 and 1951. Novi racing cars were switched from front-drive to rear-drive in 1956 and made their final appearance as an entered car in 1966.

1948 Novi

Indianapolis "500" Race Cars

When Indianapolis 500 specifications were changed dramatically to encourage a return of production-based cars for 1930, Clessie Cummins sought to enter a Cummins Diesel-powered car for 1931. After expressing concern that the heavy Duesenberg-built car might not have the speed to qualify, he was guaranteed a spot providing the car could complete a 4-lap qualifying average speed in excess of 80 mph. Driver Dave Evans qualified at 96.871. Evans then proceeded to complete the entire distance without a single pit stop, averaging 86.107 mph and completing the full 500 miles some 35 minutes after the winner had crossed the line.

1931 Cummins Diesel

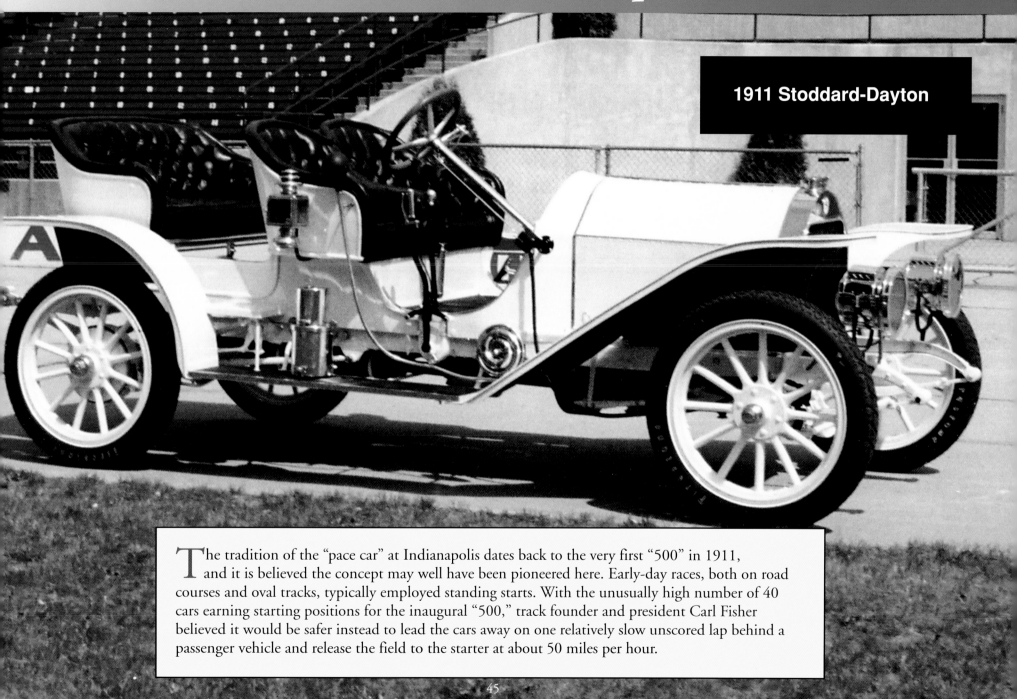

1911 Stoddard-Dayton

The tradition of the "pace car" at Indianapolis dates back to the very first "500" in 1911, and it is believed the concept may well have been pioneered here. Early-day races, both on road courses and oval tracks, typically employed standing starts. With the unusually high number of 40 cars earning starting positions for the inaugural "500," track founder and president Carl Fisher believed it would be safer instead to lead the cars away on one relatively slow unscored lap behind a passenger vehicle and release the field to the starter at about 50 miles per hour.

1966 Mercury Comet Cyclone GT

1975 Buick Century Custom

1964 Ford Mustang

1977 Oldsmobile Delta 88

1986 Chevrolet Corvette

1991 Dodge Viper RT-10

Indianapolis "500" Pace Cars

1993 Chevrolet Camaro Z28

2003 Chevrolet SSR

2002 Chevrolet Corvette

During a NASCAR test at the Indianapolis Motor Speedway in mid-August, 1993—almost exactly one year prior to the first running of the Brickyard 400—Richard Petty, who had retired at the end of the previous season, took a ceremonial lap around the track in this 1992 Pontiac Grand Prix and then turned it over to the Hall of Fame Museum.

**1992 Pontiac Grand Prix
Richard Petty**

Motorcycles

When the Indianapolis Motor Speedway was being constructed, the intent was that motorcycles would be raced and tested there in addition to automobiles. Unfortunately, motorcycle racing ended up being restricted to one day only. The original program was scheduled for Friday and Saturday (August 13 and 14, 1909), one week before the first automobile races. As luck would have it, Friday the 13th was rained out. The two-day program was then rescheduled for Saturday and Monday (no racing on Sundays in those days), but the surface of crushed rock and tar caused so many problems that the program was cancelled completely just before the final event of the first day. The brick surface put down in the fall was not conducive to motorcycle racing. One of the events held before the cancellation, a four-lap contest for the "amateur championship," was won by young Erwin G. Baker, who was still several years away from being given the nickname "Cannonball."

**1962
Manx Norton**

1909 Indian

1938 Regent

**1923
Harley-Davidson**

Entrepreneurial, motor-minded and young, William Harley and three Davidson brothers started their company in a backyard shed in 1903. This Model JD23 carries a 22-hp version of the legendary "74" 2-cylinder, twin-V engine, designed specifically for sidecar bikes. In 1923, the firm introduced the first Harleys with electric ignition and a headlight. From 1917 until 1932, Harley-Davidson offered customers a single color choice: olive drab.

Motorcycles

This Indian Motorcycle Company bike holds an in-line 4-cylinder cast-iron L-head engine. Indian engines of this type powered many winning midget race cars in the 1930s and 1940s. Note the partial leaf spring front suspension and the rear fender hinged to ease tire installation. The 1940 Indian adopted skirted fenders that gave the machine a more streamlined, speedy look.

1940 Indian

1934 Harley-Davidson 350cc Racing Bike

Nicknamed "Pea shooter," this 350cc racing bike was raced with great success by Joe Petrali, the legendary American Motorcycle Association flat track, board track and hill climb champion. Later a chief mechanic at Indianapolis; flight engineer for Howard Hughes on "The Spruce Goose," and chief official for all of the World Land Speed record attempts at the Bonneville Salt Flats in the 1960s, Petrali was the choice of AMA to be presented with its Life Membership number one.

1939 Indian

Helmets and Uniforms

Helmets, goggles, uniforms and other apparel are all part of the collection, many of the items having been donated by either the participants themselves or members of their family. A display of "helmets through the decades" has been featured in the Museum for several years.

1911

1919

1920

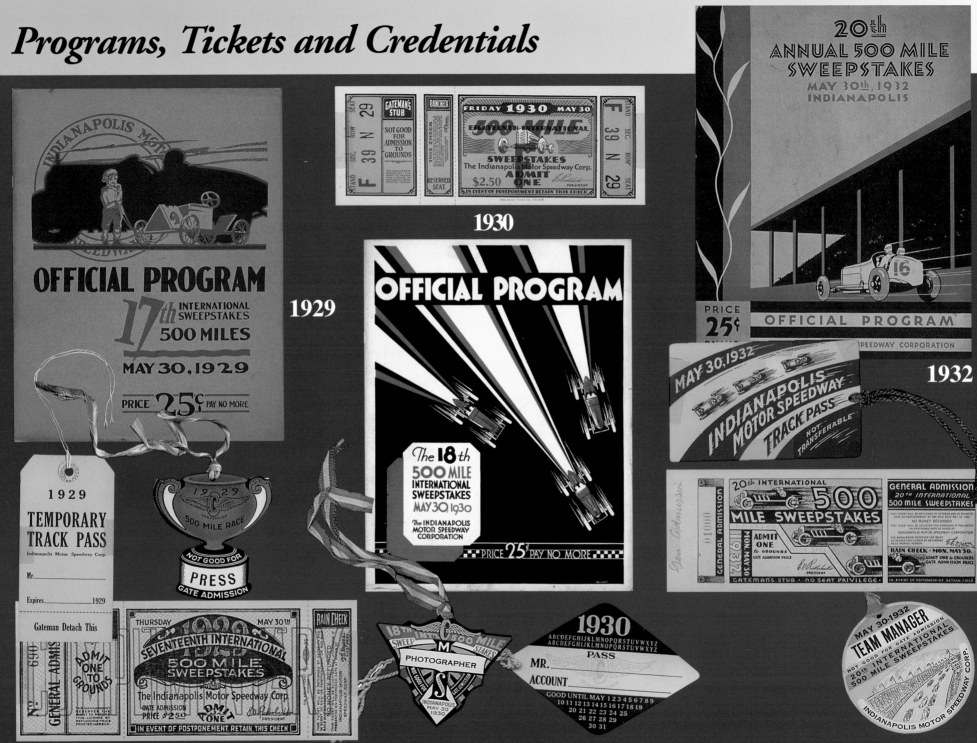

1929

1930

1932

56

1982

1994

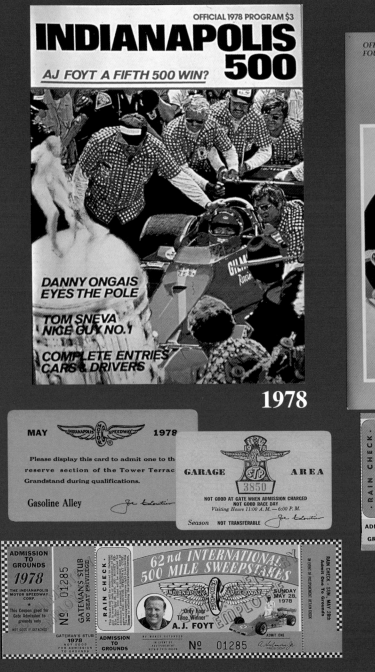

OFFICIAL 1978 PROGRAM $3

INDIANAPOLIS 500

AJ FOYT A FIFTH 500 WIN?

DANNY ONGAIS
EYES THE POLE

TOM SNEVA
NICE GUY NO.1

COMPLETE ENTRIES
CARS & DRIVERS

1978

OFFICIAL PROGRAM
FOUR DOLLARS

INDIANAPOLIS 500
THE SIXTY-SIXTH · MAY 30, 1982

"An American Tradition"

OFFICIAL PROGRAM

INDIANAPOLIS 500

EIGHT DOLLARS

Borg Warner Trophy

The BorgWarner trophy has been a part of every Indianapolis "500" victory ceremony since 1936 and is one of the most recognizable sporting event trophies in the world. It has appeared in several motion pictures. Unveiled at a dinner in New York in February 1936 and containing an estimated $10,000 worth of silver, it featured a bas-relief sculpture of every "500" winner up through 1935. Each winner was added thereafter all the way up until 1986, when the inevitable occurred and the final available space became filled. A base was added for 1987, but this too was filled by 2003, replaced now by an even larger base which should not be filled until 2034. Every winning driver between 1936 and 1987 was awarded a small bas-relief replica of the trophy mounted on a plaque. Starting in 1991, the winner has been presented with a sterling silver miniature, affectionately nicknamed "Baby Borg."

Strauss Trophy Collection

L. Strauss & Co., a prestigious Indianapolis men's clothing store began offering an award to the winner of the Indianapolis 500 from the time of the first race in 1911. For the next three decades, Strauss would commission an art collector to select a classic piece of sculpture, normally from Europe, and usually depicting speed in some form.

1919

1923

1931

60

Additional Trophies

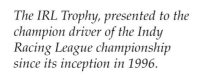

The IRL Trophy, presented to the champion driver of the Indy Racing League championship since its inception in 1996.

The U.S. Grand Prix trophy is presented to the winner of the United States Formula One Grand Prix, first held on the Indianapolis Motor Speedway road course in 2000.

The Brickyard 400 trophy, presented to every winner of the Brickyard 400 since the inaugural running in 1994.

There can hardly be a racing series in the United States that does not proclaim its most outstanding newcomer as "Rookie of the Year." Believed to have begun with baseball, it is entirely possible that the concept as applied to motorsports began in 1952 when a local meat-packing company, Stark & Wetzel, began honoring a "Rookie of the Year" for the Indianapolis 500. Although the award continues to this day, Stark & Wetzel's involvement ended and the original trophy was retired when the company was sold in 1977.

The Cobe Cup was put up in 1909 by the Chicago Automobile Club for a 300-mile road race held at Crown Point, Indiana, and won by Louis Chevrolet. When the event was not renewed for 1910, the Cup was transferred to the Indianapolis Motor Speedway for a 200-mile race, also held only once. It was transferred again to the road races at Elgin, Illinois, in 1913 and last awarded in 1920.

Leo Krauss, an Indianapolis jeweler, put up this elaborate jeweled crown for the winner of every Indianapolis 500 between 1924 and 1936, it being retired permanently by Louis Meyer, the first to win the "500" three times, in 1928, 1933 and 1936.

Peter DePaolo was presented with these two exquisite cobalt blue glass and silver vases by A.L. Block for winning the 1925 Indianapolis 500.

The massive Wheeler-Schebler trophy was commissioned from Tiffany's by industrialist Frank Wheeler, one of the four founding fathers of the Indianapolis Motor Speedway for a major event held at the track in 1909 and 1910. When management began presenting only one race per year—the "500"—this became one of several trophies to be temporarily retired. In 1914, it was revived as a special award for the leader at 400 miles, the first entrant to win it three times taking permanent possession. Former driver Harry Hartz met this requirement when cars owned by him led at 400 miles in 1930, '31 and '32.

R udolf Caracciola, the great European champion of 1935, '37 and '38, tried to qualify for the 1946 Indianapolis "500" but was seriously injured in an accident during practice. Mr. and Mrs. Tony Hulman, who had recently purchased the track, invited Caracciola and his wife to spend part of the summer at their country lodge in Terre Haute, Indiana, while he convalesced. A very close friendship was cemented and several years after Caracciola had passed away in 1959, an arrangement was made whereby the champion's entire trophy collection would be deeded to the Hall of Fame Museum.

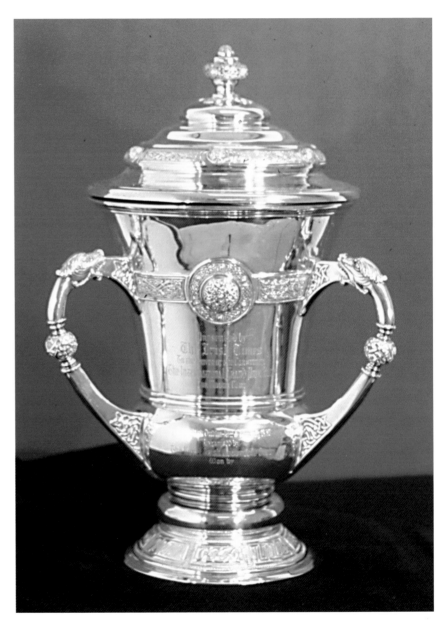

1955 winner Bob Sweikert by Ron Burton.

Arie Luyendyk pit stop by Peter Hearsey, 1991.

The Hall of Fame Museum collection includes original artwork by such renowned artists as Peter Helck, leRoy Neiman, Ken Dallison, Bernie Fuchs, Charles Fazzino, Jim Dietz, Ron Burton and William Ware, among others.

A.J.Foyt pit stop by William Ware, 1977.

1914 poster litho. by Oval & Koster.

Cover of the 2003
Brickyard 400 program
by Bernie Fuchs.

*Peter Helck, 1965. As dramatic a moment as any in Indianapolis history came in 1912
when the Italian-born American Ralph DePalma had victory snatched away from him after
leading virtually the entire race. Driving a privately owned German chain-driven
Mercedes, he had taken over the lead on the third lap and did not relinquish it until over six
hours later, being 5 1/2 laps (11 minutes) ahead of second place when a connecting rod
snapped. It punched a hole in the crankcase and proceeded to pump out all of the oil.
DePalma struggled along for a couple more laps until the car finally ground to a halt in the
fourth turn of its 199th lap, approximately one and a quarter laps from the finish. To the
amazement of the crowd, DePalma and his riding mechanic, Australian Rupert Jeffkins,
began to push the heavy car through the turn and down the home stretch to their pit.
Another entire lap would have been out of the question! It was while they still had about
another hundred yards to go that second-placed Joe Dawson finally swept by to win—as
depicted in the classic Peter Helck painting (above). The Indianapolis-built National with
which Dawson won has, like the 1911 Marmon "Wasp," been cared for throughout its life
and is on display in the Museum.*

The first three finishers in the 1911 "500" are all shown in this painting by Peter Helck, winner Ray Harroun being in number 32, runner-up Ralph Mulford in car number 33 and third place-finishing David Bruce-Brown in number 28.

Peter Helck, 1965.

Indianapolis 500 program cover, 1989, by Jim Dietz.

Jules Goux pit stop by Fred Stout.

For the 1986 Indianapolis 500 program foldout cover, artist **Bernie Fuchs** created this hauntingly realistic depiction of every one of history's multiple winners along with 1911 winner Ray Harroun. Standing left to right, each at the height of his career, are A.J. Foyt, Bobby Unser, Al Unser, Wilbur Shaw, Johnny Rutherford, Bill Vukovich, Louis Meyer, Tommy Milton, Gordon Johncock, Mauri Rose, Rick Mears and Rodger Ward.

1933 Grand Prix Poster by Geottam.

leRoy Neiman, 1963.

This dramatic scene by Michael Turner depicts the split second after Emerson Fittipladi and Al Unser, Jr., had touched wheels while battling for the lead one and a quarter laps from the end of the 1989 "500." Unser unavoidably hit the wall as Fittipaldi went on to win under the caution flag. Unser, completely uninjured, still placed second due to the distance he had covered.